DESERT TORTOISES

by Sophie Lockwood

Content Adviser: Harold K. Voris, PhD, Curator and Head,
Amphibians and Reptiles, Department of Zoology,
The Field Museum, Chicago, Illinois

THE CHILD'S WORLD®, CHANHASSEN, MINNESOTA

DESERT TORTOISES

Published in the United States of America by The Child's World®
PO Box 326 • Chanhassen, MN 55317-0326 • 800-599-READ • www.childsworld.com

Acknowledgements:

The Child's World®: Mary Berendes, Publishing Director

Editorial Directions, Inc.: E. Russell Primm, Editorial Director; Pam Rosenberg, Editor; Judith Shiffer, Assistant Editor; Caroline Wood and Rory Mabin, Editorial Assistants; Susan Hindman, Copy Editor; Emily Dolbear and Sarah E. De Capua, Proofreaders; Elizabeth Nellums, Olivia Nellums, and Daisy Porter, Fact Checkers; Tim Griffin/IndexServ, Indexer; Cian Loughlin O'Day, Photo Researcher, Linda S. Koutris, Photo Editor

The Design Lab: Kathleen Petelinsek, Art Director, Cartographer; Julia Goozen, Page Production Artist

Photos:

Cover: Glenn M. Oliver / Visuals Unlimited; frontispiece / 4: Bruce Heinemann / Photodisc / Getty Images.

Interior: Alamy Images: 5-middle and 22 (Dynamics Graphic Group / Creatas), 10 (Paul Wood), 21 (Brett Jorgensen / Stock Connection Distribution), 24 (Grady Harrison); Animals Animals / Earth Scenes: 5-top left and 8 (Gerlach Nature Photography), 16 (Paul and Joyce Berquist), 19 (Ted Levin); Corbis: 5-top right and 12 (Jonathan Blair), 5-bottom right and 29 (Gianni Dagli Orti), 5-bottom left and 36, 15 (Kennan Ward), 27 (Tom Bean), 31 (Craig Aurness), 35 (Kennan Ward); Getty Images: 2-3 (Steve Lewis / The Image Bank), 32 (Greg Vaughn / The Image Bank).

Library of Congress Cataloging-in-Publication Data

Lockwood, Sophie.
 Desert tortoises / by Sophie Lockwood.
   p. cm. — (The world of reptiles)
 Includes bibliographical references (p.   ) and index.
 ISBN 1-59296-546-6 (library bound : alk. paper)
 1. Desert tortoise—Juvenile literature. I. Title.
 QL666.C584L63 2006
 597.92'4—dc22   2005024788

TABLE OF CONTENTS

Chapter One

In the Mojave Desert

It is April in the Mojave Desert in California. Joshua trees stand among scruffy creosote bush and prickly pear cactus. It has been a good winter, and wildflowers now paint the land bright yellow, red, and purple.

A female desert tortoise slowly digs a 6-foot-long (1.8-meter-long) summer home. The soil is dry, sandy, and easy to dig. The tortoise has plenty of burrow-building experience. A desert tortoise usually has several active burrows, depending on its age and where it lives. There are winter burrows that stretch up to 30 feet (9 m) long. Summer burrows are shorter. Desert tortoises are forever digging new burrows and abandoning old ones. This burrow is just one of many that this tortoise has dug during her lifetime.

The area in which a tortoise lives is called its home range. The average home range of a tortoise measures from 27 to 131 acres (10 to 53 hectares). Our female tortoise will spend her entire life within

Did You Know?
Desert tortoises are found in the southwestern United States and northern Mexico. They live in the Mojave and Sonoran deserts.

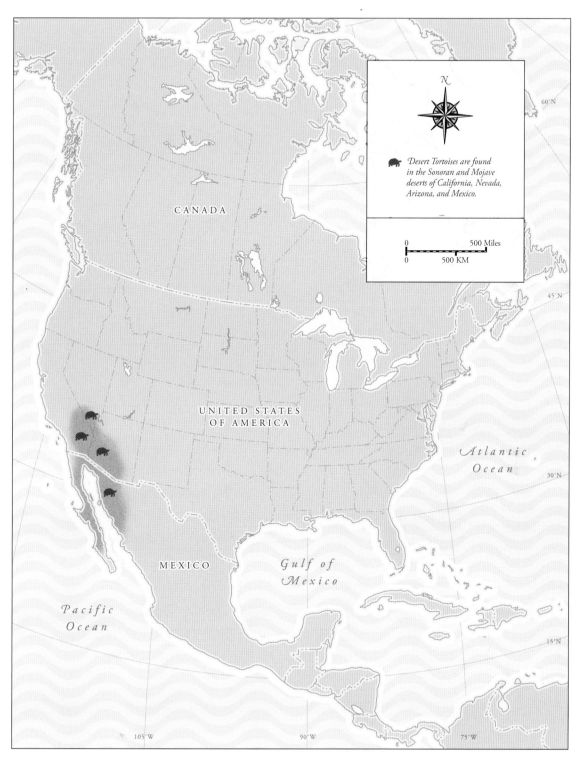

This map shows the range of desert tortoise habitats.

her home range. She will dig burrows, feed, find mates, build nests, and lay her eggs there. She knows her home range well and recognizes local landmarks. An oddly shaped Joshua tree, a jutting rock, and a dry riverbed are her neighborhood.

The new summer burrow offers protection from the desert heat. Desert tortoise burrows have half-moon shaped roofs. The arched shape matches their dome-shaped shells.

A desert tortoise emerges from its burrow in the Mojave Desert.

When the tortoise changes burrows, her old winter burrow becomes home to some other animal. Kit foxes, burrowing owls, and snakes take over empty desert tortoise burrows. They are among the many creatures that inhabit the desert.

Near the burrow, a Mojave rattlesnake suns himself on a rock, and a chuckwalla lizard wedges itself under a stone ridge. Rattlesnakes, chuckwallas, and tortoises are all reptiles and cold-blooded. They need the sun's heat to warm their bodies.

Our desert tortoise thrives in the springtime desert. She munches on flowers and the fruit of the prickly pear cactus. She dines each morning on purple lupines, sage, and poppies. She doesn't have to drink water because the plants she eats provide all the liquid she needs.

The sun rises high in the sky. Heat drifts off the land in waves. Our female tortoise takes to the shelter of her burrow. She avoids the heat of the day because it makes her overheat. The burrow is cooler and slightly humid. She eases herself down for a nap. After millions of years, the desert tortoise has learned that the best way to beat the desert heat is to take a siesta.

Did You Know?
A desert tortoise only drinks water when desert plants dry up. To collect water, it digs shallow basins in the soil at the bottom of slopes. The tortoise returns to the basins when it rains and drinks the rainwater that pools in them.

Chapter Two

Strong Legs and Hard Shells

If desert tortoises look like prehistoric creatures in miniature, it is because they are. Desert tortoises have roamed the drier regions of Earth for more than 67 million years. The species survived because desert tortoise bodies adapted to hot, dry climates that would kill many other animals.

Desert tortoises belong to the reptile family called Testudinidae. There are many different types of tortoises, ranging from small desert and gopher tortoises to the gigantic Galapagos and Aldabran tortoises. They are often thought of as turtles that live on land, but because they live on land, they have developed special characteristics suited for land life. For example, tortoises do not have webbed feet like most turtles.

The desert tortoise's obvious physical traits are its shell and strong legs. A tortoise is protected top and bottom by

The largest populations of gopher tortoises are found in Florida and Georgia. They are one of the desert tortoise's closest relatives.

Did You Know?

The desert tortoise's closest relatives are the gopher tortoises found in the southeastern United States, the Texas tortoise found in Texas and Mexico, and the Bolson tortoise, found only in Mexico. The Bolson tortoise was discovered in 1959, and it is already critically **endangered** in the wild.

its shell. The upper shell is called the **carapace.** On a desert tortoise, the carapace is domed and brown, olive green, yellowish, or black in color. The carapace has bony scales, called **scutes** that look like armor. In fact, that is what they are. Scutes form the patterns that make tortoise shells so attractive. The under shell is called the **plastron.** It is flat and pale brown to yellowish in color. A hard bony ridge holds the plastron to the carapace.

A tortoise's legs are designed for desert living. The rear limbs are thick columns of muscle and bone. They are the same shape as an elephant's legs but much smaller. The front

A desert tortoise rests inside its shell. Like many tortoises, desert tortoises have high, domed shells.

limbs have claws for digging and protective scales. When frightened, a tortoise draws in its head, tail, and limbs. The front limbs cover and protect the head. An enemy sees only the shell and the hard, scaly forelimbs.

Like most desert creatures, a tortoise can survive with very little water. Most of the water it consumes comes from the plants it eats. The tortoise's body removes the water from the plants and stores it in a large bladder. Humans rid their bodies of excess water and other liquid waste by **urinating.** Desert tortoises save the water in their bladders. They also have the ability to turn the chemicals and salts in their urine into solid waste. On the rare occasions when it does rain in the desert, the tortoise drinks a lot of water from the temporary pools of rainwater that form. The old urine in its bladder is then excreted along with the solidified wastes. Most of the fresh rainwater the tortoise drinks refills the bladder.

THE TORTOISE LIFE CYCLE

Female tortoises cannot reproduce until they are mature, usually between fifteen and twenty years old. Most desert animals have life spans shorter than that. Coyotes, ravens, and badgers in the wild usually

Desert Tortoise Fast Facts
(*Gopherus agassizii*)
Adult length: Carapace is 9 to 15 inches (23 to 38 cm) long
Weight: 8 to 15 pounds (3.6 to 6.8 kilograms)
Coloration: Brown, olive green, yellow, or black carapace; pale brown or yellow plastron
Range: Sonoran and Mojave deserts of California, Nevada, Arizona, and Mexico
Reproduction: 2 to 3 **clutches** each year, 3 to 14 eggs per nest
Diet: Grasses, wildflowers, herbs, cactus flowers, and fruits
U.S. status: Threatened

only live about fifteen years. To survive to maturity, a desert tortoise must avoid **predators,** humans, and disease. It must survive drought, cold, floods, and wildfires.

A female tortoise lays a small clutch (three to fourteen eggs) in a nest. The number of eggs depends on the size of the tortoise. Small females lay fewer eggs than large ones. The eggs, about the size of Ping-Pong balls, develop in 70 to 120 days. The length of time it takes for eggs to develop is strongly influenced by the climate. Some eggs will remain unhatched until after the winter ends—if they survive that long. Gila monsters, kit foxes, coyotes, and badgers often raid tortoise nests and feast on the high-protein eggs.

Hatchlings are small, and their shells are very soft. They make a nice snack for a hungry meat eater. Their growth rate is extremely slow, only about 0.25 to 0.33 inch (0.64 to 0.84 cm) per year. Desert tortoises must survive for six years before they are big enough and their shells hard enough to discourage most predators. In addition to coyotes, foxes, and badgers, ravens, roadrunners, skunks, and even snakes prey on **juvenile** tortoises. About 99 percent of eggs, hatchlings, and juveniles die before adulthood. That means only one egg out of fifteen to twenty nests will become an adult desert tortoise.

Desert tortoises do not take care of their young. Few hatchlings survive to adulthood.

As adults, desert tortoises measure 9 to 15 inches long (23 to 38 cm). The length is measured along the carapace. It does not include the head, neck, and tail. Adults weigh from 8 to 15 pounds (3.6 to 6.8 kg). Size and growth depend on the amount and quality of food the tortoise eats. A diet rich in proteins produces a larger tortoise at a faster pace.

Even older desert tortoises must keep an eye out for badgers, bobcats, golden eagles, and coyotes. The adult tortoise's hard shell does not keep determined predators from enjoying a tortoise meat dinner.

Desert coyotes are light gray or tan and have black tips on their tails. They sometimes eat tortoises.

A KEYSTONE SPECIES

Desert tortoises are considered a keystone species of their environments. A keystone species is any animal or plant on which other animals or plants depend heavily for survival. One way that tortoises help their environment is by digging burrows, which puts air into the soil and encourages plant growth. Healthy plants feed and provide shelter for many other creatures.

In addition, desert tortoises are plant eaters. Like all **herbivores,** they digest much of their food and expel some seeds and solid waste. The waste acts as fertilizer for desert soil. The waste also spreads seeds to new locations and encourages new plants to grow.

Perhaps more important, empty tortoise burrows don't stay empty for long. As the tortoises move out, other desert creatures move in. Snakes, kit foxes, burrowing owls, spiders, kangaroo rats, and other underground residents thrive in the protection of abandoned tortoise burrows. Loss of desert tortoises throughout their natural range would injure populations of other animals that live in tortoise burrows. The survival of this ancient reptile allows the survival of many other desert species.

Would You Believe? Desert tortoises that make it to adulthood can live eighty to one hundred years.

Chapter Three

A Lonely Life

A desert tortoise spends nearly 95 percent of its life underground. It's safe. It's cool. It's home.

In early spring, a tortoise emerges to feed on the fresh plants blooming in its home range. A typical tortoise might leave the burrow in mid-morning, eat until mid-afternoon, then return home to sleep.

Summer brings a dramatic change in tortoise behavior. During the hottest months, tortoises are active only around dawn and dusk. Their active times change according to the weather. After a rain, desert landscapes often change from barren to flower covered overnight. Summer rains encourage tortoises to check out newly sprouting plants. On the other hand, a very dry, hot spell will discourage tortoises from leaving home at all.

Winter is a time when all reptiles would suffer if they did not behave in ways that allow them to regulate their

Would You Believe?
A desert tortoise sleeps for long periods in winter and summer. Winter sleeping—hibernation—allows the tortoise to avoid freezing temperatures. But its burrow is still very cold, and the cold temperatures slow the tortoise's metabolism. This allows it to survive during a time when there is very little food available because they require very little energy while hibernating. Summer sleeping—estivation—lets the tortoise avoid long, very hot, dry spells.

body temperature. They cannot control their body temperatures internally. A bitter winter outside would freeze them to death if they did not hibernate. Hibernation is one behavior that allows tortoises and other reptiles to regulate body temperature. They sleep through the worst of the winter below the frost line.

A desert tortoise munches on beavertail cactus in the Mojave Desert. Most of the water the tortoise needs comes from the plants that it eats.

Tortoises ready themselves for their sleeping season by building long, deep burrows. A winter burrow may be as much as five times longer than the summer burrow. Occasionally, many tortoises will gather in one deep burrow and hibernate as a group. For a species that normally spends its time alone, a group sleepover is surprising behavior.

POPULATIONS AND HABITATS

There are three distinct desert tortoise populations: the Mojave Desert group, the Sonoran Desert group, and a group that lives in the Mexican states of Sonora and Sinaloa. These groups do not mix. They cannot migrate great distances and have adapted to the specific environments in which they live.

The Mojave population digs deep, roomy burrows. They live in the creosote scrub, an area of desert speckled with scruffy-looking bushes. They prefer sandy flats, washes, canyons, and rocky foothills for burrow digging. Rocks or bushes hide burrow locations.

The Sonoran Desert environment has different soil. It discourages desert tortoises from excavating the type of burrows found in the Mojave. Paloverde and saguaro cactus

fill the landscape. In this region, desert tortoises usually dig very shallow burrows on rocky hillsides. If a natural, shallow cave is found, so much the better. It saves the tortoise the trouble of having to dig through hard, crusty soil.

The desert tortoise is the largest reptile that lives in the Mojave Desert.

Sonora and Sinaloa border the Gulf of California. The unpopulated regions are dotted with thorn scrub. Much of the flat, coastal land is used to grow sugarcane or cotton. Inland, the land rises into the Sierra Madre range. Desert tortoises do not live above 3,500 feet (1,068 m). They make their homes in the rocky foothills of the Sierra Madres.

SOCIAL BEHAVIOR

Desert tortoises usually live alone. They see each other as they pass through one another's home ranges. Head bobs and assorted hisses, grunts, and whoops pass for communication.

The Sonoran desert, in the foothills of the Sierra Madres, is home to desert tortoises. The animals dig shallow burrows in the rocky hillsides.

Mating draws tortoises together in late spring to early fall. Males meet to establish which tortoise gets to mate and which runs—well, creeps—away. Two males face each other in shell-to-shell combat. The stronger male uses the bony horn on his plastron to force his opponent onto his back. Battle over. The winner goes after the female. The loser desperately uses his head, neck, and forelimbs to turn himself right side up. If he cannot do so, he will die.

Once the male and female mate, the female digs a nest for her eggs. She urinates heavily in the area, then digs. As she lays the eggs, she urinates again, and then covers the nest with dirt. The urine has a strong scent. Many scientists believe that the female does this to fool predators. The urine may also prevent the eggs from drying out.

Tortoises do not generally protect their eggs, yet one scientist once saw a strange sight. A Gila monster began digging at a tortoise nest to eat the eggs. The tortoise mother attacked and forced the Gila monster away. Because the Gila monster's bite carries deadly poison, the tortoise could have been killed. Her only weapons were a bobbing head and a loud hiss.

Chapter Four

The Spirit of the People

The people of the Southwest tell this tale of the tortoise and the jackrabbit:

A jackrabbit bragged about his quickness to the desert animals.

"I have never yet been beaten in a race," said he. "When I run at full speed, no one can beat me. Who will take the challenge?" The coyote, the fox, and the roadrunner all refused.

The desert tortoise said quietly, "I will."

"That is a good joke," said the jackrabbit. "You do not have a chance. You are too slow."

"Keep up your bragging until you've lost," answered the tortoise. "Shall we race?"

So a path was planned and a start was made. The jackrabbit darted out of sight almost at once. He soon stopped and took a nap in the warm desert sun. He knew the tortoise could never catch up. The tortoise plodded steadily onward. When

Jackrabbits can reach speeds of up to 40 miles (64 km) per hour.

the jackrabbit woke up, he saw the tortoise near the finish line. He could not catch up in time to win the race.

Native people of the Southwest saw much to admire in the slow desert tortoise. People first arrived in the deserts of southwestern North America about ten thousand years ago. The desert tortoise was already there. The people saw that the tortoise offered clues to survival in the harsh desert climate. Tortoises moved slowly, worked in the cool parts of the day, and slept through the worst of the heat.

The newly arrived clans hunted the tortoise for food. Scientists and historians have found tortoise bones and shells by ancient campfires that date back many thousands of years.

But these ancient people did not just kill tortoises for their meat. Tribal life took advantage of all that the animals could provide. Tortoise shells became scoops, bowls, cooking pots, seed holders, and ladles. Bones and parts of shell were crafted into necklaces and bracelets. The Yavapai people ground the shells of desert tortoises into powder that was used for medicine. They believed the shell powder cured stomachaches and other ills.

Did You Know?
In World War II, Navajo people served the military as Code Talkers. They passed information about the movement and arms of the enemy using the Navajo language. The word "tank" was *chay-da-gahi*—the Navajo term for "desert tortoise." The code, based on the Navajo language, was never broken during the war.

Many native cultures still use tortoise shells to make ceremonial rattles, knee-clappers, and drums. The top and bottom shells are bound together, and the space in between is filled with stones. The Hopi attach tortoise knee-clappers at the knees for many traditional dances, such as the bean ritual. As the dancers move, the shells knock together and make a clapping sound. Tortoise shell drums of different sizes create different tones. The drums are an important part of traditional native music.

A young Hopi girl prepares to participate in the Butterfly Dance. Native Americans often used tortoise bones and shells to make jewelry and musical instruments.

TORTOISE ART

Ancient people admired the tortoise for its lifestyle. They painted tortoise symbols on rattles, drums, and clothing. They wove symbols of the tortoise into baskets and used it to decorate pottery.

Although stone carvings rarely picture tortoises, there is one site where such carvings still exist. They can be seen at the Valley of Fire State Park in Nevada. Cave paintings of tortoises can be viewed in ancient ruins throughout the Mojave Desert. The ancient Mayans of Mexico's Yucatan Peninsula believed that the tortoise's round shape represented time passing. Many Mayan calendars bore the shape and design of the tortoise. In Mayan astrology, the desert tortoise had its own constellation. The Chemehuevi culture claimed that the tortoise represented the spirit of its people. They told myths honoring the tortoise because the creature accepted its fate in life—a death with dignity. The Chemehuevi people respected the tortoise's virtues of patience, endurance, and courage.

To the Cahita people, the tortoise was part villain. The Yavapai told of the desert tortoise as a stranger in their midst. The Seri of ancient Mexico called the desert tortoise *ziix hehet cquiij*—"the thing that sits in bushes." In native folklore, the tortoise is a symbol for long life. Some creation myths state that a tortoise shell is the foundation of Earth.

Native people hunted and used desert tortoises. However, they did not abuse the tortoise. They did not take tortoises as pets or destroy their homes. It was only when the Southwest became settled that the lives of desert tortoises became unsettled. Modern humans and the ancient tortoise could not share the desert.

Visitors to the ancient Mayan city of Copán in western Honduras can see this stone tortoise sculpture.

Chapter Five

Humans and Desert Tortoises

Desert tortoises are so easy to catch that humans have done so for thousands of years. Tortoises are slow moving and good eating. That's not a combination that leads to survival. Still, it wasn't the native people of the desert that caused problems for desert tortoises. Those problems began more recently.

The greatest threats to desert tortoises come from humans moving into the desert. One hundred years ago, the desert was a place to pass through on the way to the California coast. Today, it is home to big cities, golf courses, and health spas. That development proved unhealthy for desert tortoises.

The movement of humans into a wildlife habitat is called encroachment. Encroachment can take many forms. For example, people move to desert communities and try to convert scrub desert to green lawns. In doing

Human activity, such as mining, contributes to the loss of desert tortoise habitat.

A sign warns drivers to be on the lookout for desert tortoises on the road.

so, they deprive tortoises and other desert animals of their natural environment and food supply. Encroachment also comes from a network of roads. The meeting of trucks and tortoises leaves tortoises dead beside the highways. An increased number of people produces an increased amount of garbage. Waste dump sites attract ravens—one of the tortoise's natural enemies. In this case, encroachment not only pollutes the habitat, it also increases the predator population.

Desert land is also used for recreation and cattle grazing. For creatures that live underground—like the desert tortoise—these are dangerous activities. An off-road vehicle crushes underground burrows, often with the animals in them. Dune buggies kill plant life that desert tortoises eat. They often run over tortoises and injure them. A thirty-minute ride can cause damage that will take years to repair. Grazing cattle crush burrows and trample the few plants they don't eat. They compete with tortoises for food.

Even worse, people have taken tortoises from the wild and turned them into pets. This is against the law in California, Arizona, Utah, and Nevada. Wild creatures belong in the wild, and tortoises make very boring pets. They live a very long time—usually longer than the humans who take them. What happens then?

Unfortunately, some people think they can just put a tortoise back into the wild and it will thrive. This is not true—and it is also against the law. Pet tortoises carry diseases back to the native tortoise population. The most dangerous is upper respiratory distress syndrome, a lung disease that kills tortoises. To prevent pet tortoises from being returned to the wild, state **conservation** groups have developed desert tortoise adoption programs. These programs keep pet and wild tortoises separate—and safe.

THE FUTURE OF THE DESERT TORTOISE

Scientists continue to study ways to save the threatened desert tortoise. One problem desert tortoises face is an exceptionally slow reproduction and growth rate. Scientists can't make female tortoises lay eggs at a younger age, but they can save the eggs from becoming a coyote's dinner. Eggs are removed from the wild and hatched in laboratories. The hatchlings are raised in "natural" conditions and fed high-protein foods to help them grow more quickly. The plan is to improve the survival rate from egg to adult, a rate that now stands at 1 percent.

Public and private preserves secure home ranges

Some desert tortoise conservation groups raise young desert tortoises and return them to the wild when they are older, larger, and less likely to be eaten by predators.

for desert tortoise populations. In these ranges, the tortoise is safe. Though they still face predators, flash floods, drought, and unreliable food supplies, they do not have to cope with their worst enemy—humans.

Scientists are also investigating how **alien** plants affect tortoise populations. Native plants in a tortoise's home range might include sage, creosote bush, and cacti. Seeds from

The desert tortoise is an important part of its environment. Scientists are working to ensure the survival of both the desert tortoise and its desert habitat.

plant species that do not belong in the desert arrive there and flourish. Red brome, cheatgrass, and Sahara mustard grass are alien plant species that do not belong in southwestern deserts. They throw off nature's balance, taking growing room away from native grasses and shrubs. Scientists have discovered that tortoises will eat some alien plants, but not others. Nonetheless, reducing the opportunities for alien plants to invade tortoise territory is the best plan.

Is it a natural part of life for a species to become **extinct**? To a certain extent, yes. Many animal species have become extinct due to natural causes—massive volcanoes erupting, meteors striking Earth, or even drastic changes in weather. A species' extinction because of human carelessness, however, is not acceptable. This is particularly true when the species is a keystone species.

Losing the desert tortoise might also mean losing the plants that are nourished and seeded by tortoise waste. It might also mean losing the animals that live in tortoise burrows and those that feed on tortoise eggs and hatchlings. Nature's balance is like a stack of dominoes. Push one over, and they all fall over. Scientists and other concerned people are working hard to make sure the desert tortoise isn't the domino that pushes the desert environment to its doom.

Glossary

alien (AY-lee-uhn) foreign

carapace (KAR-uh-payss) a turtle's upper shell

clutches (KLUHCH-es) groups of eggs laid in nests

conservation (kon-sur-VAY-shuhn) the act of saving or preserving some aspect of wildlife

endangered (ehn-DAYN-jurd) threatened with extinction

extinct (ek-STINGKT) no longer in existence

herbivores (HUR-buh-vorz) plant eaters

juvenile (JOO-vuh-nuhl) a young animal, like a human toddler

plastron (PLASS-truhn) the under shell of a turtle

predators (PRED-uh-turz) animals that hunt and kill other animals for food

scutes (SKOOTS) bony scales on the exterior of desert tortoises

urinating (YOOR-uh-nate-ing) ridding a body of liquid waste

For More Information

Watch It

A Violent Eden. VHS (Alexandria, Va., National Geographic, 1997).

Read It

Cornett, James W. *The Desert Tortoise.* Palm Springs, Calif.: Palm Springs Desert Museum, 2002.

Lazaroff, David, and Preston Neel (illustrator). *Correctamundo!: Prickly Pete's Guide to Desert Facts and Cactifracts.* Tucson: Arizona-Sonora Desert Museum Press, 2001.

Look It Up

Visit our home page for lots of links about desert tortoises: *http://www.childsworld.com/links*

Note to Parents, Teachers, and Librarians: We routinely verify our Web links to make sure they are safe, active sites—so encourage your readers to check them out!

The Animal Kingdom
Where Do Desert Tortoises Fit In?

Kingdom: Animal
Phylum: Chordata
Class: Reptilia
Order: Chelonia

Family: Testudinidae (tortoises and turtles)
Genus: Gopherus
Species: agassizii

Index

About the Author

Sophie Lockwood is a former teacher and a longtime writer. She writes textbooks, newspaper articles, and magazine articles. Sophie enjoys writing about animals and their habits. The most interesting part of her research, Sophie says, is learning how scientists apply their knowledge to save endangered species. She lives with her husband in the foothills of the Blue Ridge Mountains.